The Real King Solomon's Mines

A Guide to the Ancient Mines of Zimbabwe

Geoffrey Alp

Copyright © 2020 Geoffrey Alp

All rights reserved.

Revision date 12 December 2020.

DEDICATION

To my parents who loved Rhodesia now Zimbabwe and who took the time
to teach us the true treasures of Zimbabwe – its rich history.

ACKNOWLEDGMENTS

King Solomons Mines by Sir H. Rider Haggard
Southern Rhodesia Geological surveys
Rhodesian Geological surveys
The Goldfields of Mashonaland by A.R. Sawyer
Mary Lippert Letters
The Eldorado of The Ancients by Carl Peters
Numerous mine reports

THE MINES

Along time ago ancient miners worked in mines long before white men or Europeans arrived in Rhodesia (now Zimbabwe).

The story by Allan Quartermaine still stirs the imaginations of millions but what if it were true. Not the place names but the mines being real. Well the study of the ancient mines in Rhodesia (now Zimbabwe)shows the mines were very real.

This is a study of those mines, hundreds of them where tons of gold and copper was dug out the earth by the "ancients".

26	The Hero Mine	Kadoma
27	The Hope Mine	Kadoma
27	The Gladstone Reef	Harare
28	The Old Workings Reef	Harare
28	The Antelope Mine Reefs	Kezi District
29	The Siren Mine	Lower Gweru
30	The Crescent Mine	Chinhoyi
30	The Gondia Mine	Chinhoyi
31	The ANZAC Mine	Chinhoyi
31	Comyn Ranch cluster	Lower Gweru
31	Leopard Mine Group	Lower Gweru
32	Gothic, Pagamesa and Do Me Good Mines.	Lower Gweru
33	The Geldenhys Deep Mine	Lower Gweru
34	The Gold Enough Mine	Lower Gweru
34	The Odd Fellow Mine	Lower Gweru
34	Blue Jacket Mine Botswana	Tati
35	Nourse Mine	Fort Victoria
36	Summerton Mine	Masivingo
37	The Fortunate Mine	Masivingo
38	The Suffolk Mine	Masivingo
38	The Cornwallis Mine	Masivingo
39	The Cold Punch Mine	Belingwe
40	B and B Mine	Belingwe
40	C Mine	Belingwe
40	The Blue Bell Mine	Belingwe
41	The Bunyip Claims	Belingwe
43	The Rosina Claims	Belingwe
43	The Sirus Mine	Shangani
44	The New Eclipse mine	Shangani
45	Annies Luck Mine	Shangani
46	The Blighty Mine	Shangani
46	The Chromate Mine	Shangani
47	Shamrock and Rose of Sharon Mine	Hunter Road
47	The Camelia Mine	Kwe Kwe
48	The Sebakwe Mine	Kwe Kwe
48	The Kings Mine	Kwe Kwe
48	The Owl Mine	Kadoma
49	The Cusco mine	Lower Gweru
51	The Elephant Mine	Lower Gweru

Authors Notes

The records of ancient miners activity comes from many sources, however it wasn't historians or archaeologists recording these records but rather mine inspectors. As a result their notes are rather brief. For the purposes of recording these, I have only used mine reports where ancient activity was specifically noted, as over 90% of the gold mines in Rhodesia were founded on ancient workings. Carbon dating of remains shows that mining was well established at about 600 AD some 300 to 400 years before the Zimbabwe style stone structures were built. However the last recording of ancient mining activity was near Sinoia or Chinhoyi which was in the early 1800's.

However this was attributed to the Portuguese wishing to exploit the old gold mines rather than them being the instigators of the ancient goldmining activity.

I am sure that with time many more instances of ancient mining activity could be found, but the limiting factor is the acquisition of the old geological reports which is very costly and they are hard to find.

King Lobengula's own gold mine and stamping mill.

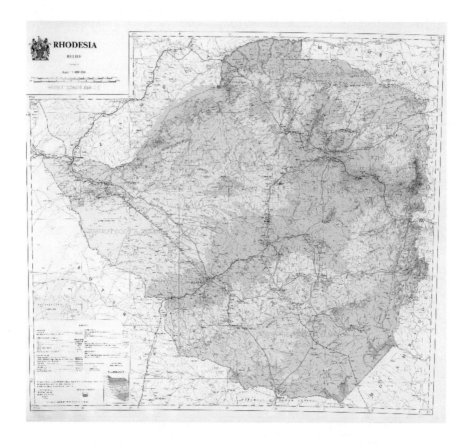

THE GOLD MINES

Early writings from Portuguese, namely Izidoro Correia Pereira who was a Zambezi trader described the early mining activities in a paper published in Lisbon in 1857.

One has to note here that the furthest inland the Portuguese had penetrated by evidence were their forts come trading stations, one seen in the picture below which was on the Angwa river.

Loc: 17.01.54 S and 29.57.48 E

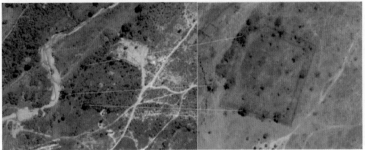

Angwa River Portuguese forts.

There was also another trading station near Chakari called Maramuca[1] where an ivory figurine of the Virgin Mary was found[2].

Other claims, like there was a Portuguese presence at Dhlo Dhlo have somewhat been discounted as being looted items from a battle between the later inhabitants of Dhlo Dhlo and the Portuguese. These included the two cannons. The reported trading fort in the Kwe Kwe area still remains to be found.

Pereira writings go on to describe the dynasty of Hera at Shurushuru, Mwenzi and Nyamakanga, with the Devera named as "discoverers and workers"[3]. The evidence from the distribution of the Zimbabwe style ruins and the location of noted workings given in this book shows that the mines were probably operating for hundreds of years prior to the Portuguese arrival. Secondly anyone making claims to have known names of the early ancient miners and tribes some 200 years back is ludicrous. There have been claims by so called historians of the name of an African king some 600 years ago, all based on word of mouth and whimsical thinking.

To confirm the erroneous thinking one has to note the earliest European mines opened in the Kadoma area in 1901, made note that the area between

---

[1] Maramuca was excavated by Peter Garlake.

[2] Zim Field Guides - Web resources.

[3] Anne Kritzinger

Hartley Hill and Kwe Kwe was devoid of human habitation and the European miners had great difficulty in finding workers. Yet 43 years before a Portuguese trader named these nonexistent people. An early Portuguese (1897) map shows scant names and villages and the only known European mines were around Hartley.

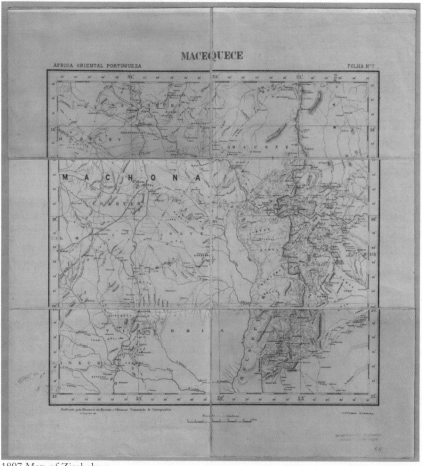

1897 Map of Zimbabwe

To try to place Pereira's gold mines by name as extending any further than local areas around Portuguese forts is unreliable, one could argue that in Zimbabwe gold is found within 100 miles of any location is probably a good fit and the truth. One also has to understand that the main means of getting around was by foot on paths that wound through and over hills and rivers. One is also reminded that the only record of place names was based on verbal communication before the 1550's. (A good example is Guelo, Gwalo, Gwelo, Gweru all names changes in the last 150 years, so what

8

would happen over say 500 years?)

Another early Portuguese writer noted and quoted a whole list of places and tribes in Zimbabwe but never left the safety of Sofala on the Mozambique coast. It was all word of mouth from travelers.

Another map from around 1700 shows the interior almost devoid of places with Dambarare one of the few named villages.

Gonçalo da Silveira has also been named as one of the first Europeans to venture into Monomatapa, however it is reported he never got further inland than the junction of Mzingezi and Zambezi rivers.

Another early map of Zimbabwe

So given the maps as being reliable proof, much of the Portuguese claims of early colonization are overstated but certainly they made inroads around the areas of Dambarare, Masapa and Luanze (1599).

The Portuguese had however noted as early as the 1500's of the Kingdom on Monomatapa. There is an ongoing opinion that the gold mining and iron implement making was a Monomatapa cultural activity.

Many authors have tried to link the gold, tin and iron ore mining to the many ruins[4] However there are many mines nowhere near any ruin and smelting also took place in caves and other areas far from ruins.

To obtain the information used in this book I have scoured many early mining reports, which are by their nature extremely rare and in many instances the reports did not disclose any information about the early mines

---

[4] There are ancient mines found that are nowhere near any ruins.

or any finds.

1. THE GLOBE, PHOENIX AND GAIKA MINES.

Located in Kwe Kwe west of the main town center the Globe and Phoenix gold reefs were uncovered by ancient miners. The Gaika mine is further south of the town center was also part of their diggings.

At the Gaika workings the ancient miners dug out an astonishing amount of gold and gold ore with their workings stretching some 3000 feet[5] long and 150 feet wide. The maximum depth reached by the ancients was 66 feet. Using a standard weight per ton of crushed quartz of 1.4 tons to cubic meter the amount of gold bearing quartz is 713,584 tons of gold ore. The Globe and Phoenix, Gaika mines were founded on magnesite (dolomite) and tale magnesite schist. The gold was deposited in a belt of shattering which was continually auriferous at the surface. The gold ore was associated with pyrite and stibnite with an occasional antimonial deposit.

The ore was very rich at the surface running at 36 dwt [6] per ton of ore mined. This would have resulted in 39 tons of pure gold. However using the later quantity of ore mined ratio to gold, the ancient miners would have processed 278,160 ounces of gold and produced a minimum 10 tons of pure gold. This is however speculation but gives one an idea of the richness of the mines.
One could also use the earliest reported tonnage to ration where in 1900 some 30,554 tons of ore were processed yielding 21,646 ounces of gold. The Phoenix mine was pegged by Edward Pearson in April 1894 on ground where the ancient miners worked two parallel reefs some 400 feet in length. In the same year the Globe mine was also pegged on ancient workings. long and to 36 feet on the one reef and 125 feet on the other. This would have yielded 357,142 tons of ore at the standard conversion rate of 1.4. These were 665 feet long and 340 feet on a parallel reef to a depth of 88 feet. The mining reports also noted the acquisition of the John Bull claims a few years later. While these mines were being opened up and developed they didn't produce in the years of the 1896 Rebellion and the South African Boer War.

---

[5] 3000 feet is roughly one kilometer.

[6] dwt is a penny weight with 20 penny weights to a troy ounce.

In comparison the world's richest mine , the Muruntau Mine in Uzbekistan produced 2,600,000 ounces of gold in 2016. The mine is however 3.5 kilometers by 2.5 kilometers and over 650 meters deep.

The old plan gives the locations of the early reefs and position in comparison to the town itself. In the aerial photograph the Phoenix reef is located at the bottom of the opencast area with the Globe reefs at the wider top portion of the open cut.

In the aerial photograph of the Gaika Mine the whole of the open cast section is more or less what was mined by the ancient miners with the length being some 3,000 feet long and a width of 150 feet.

Phoenix Mine

Layout of the Globe Phoenix and Gaika Mines is on page 53.

2.   ARDPATRICK MINE

The Ardpatrick Mine lies 3.7 miles east of Kwe Kwe and north of the airfield. It now found in amongst a number of suburbs but in its day was 1500 feet of north, south workings. The reef dipped east at 22 degrees. The ore body was gold impregnated quartz running at 7.7 dwt per ton. Due to its closeness to a small rivulet the workings ran into the water table and workings were only conducted in dryer periods. The mine was pegged on ancient workings.

Ardpatrick Mine

3. BELL MINE

The mine was pegged on ancient workings, which it seems that the ancient miners removed the best portions of the reef leaving a rather refractory ore, which was mixed with sulphides of antimony and arsenic. The nature of the mineral deposits here lead to the question of how and what knowledge the ancient miners had to identify complex minerals in situ?

The early European miners had to crush, heat and then use mercury amalgam to drop out the gold, yet the ancient miners had none of this technology.

The ancients certainly knew how to recognize gold in situ and also gold ores. To oxidize the sulphides off one has to maintain a hot temperature for an extended period of time usually hours. This drives off the sulphides and allows the gold to form small particles of gold silver mix.

Bell Mine

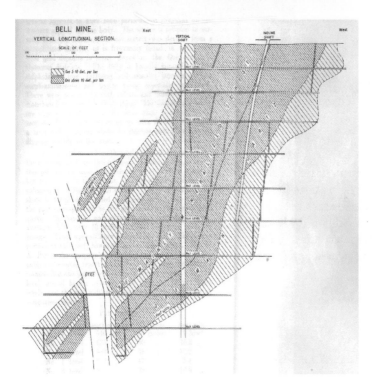

13

4.   SKIPPER COPPER MINE

The mine lies west of Kwe Kwe at Loc: 18.51.21 S and 29.35.17 E and is adjacent to the Gokwe road. The ancient miners opened up and area that is roughly as we see it today. The original workings were 800 feet and 200 feet wide. The ancient miners had gone down about 55 feet. The copper values ran at about 3.5% in copper glance. This is not particularly rich but the fact that the ancient miners were able to convert the ore to copper is significant.

To obtain copper or as the ancient miners would have done is to roast the copper glance, however it is uncertain if they used any concentration methods like grinding it and adding it to water as a primitive floatation method then heating the ore in a furnace to make blister copper.

We know from articles about the Egyptians was that copper was also found in Punt or Ophir and returned to Egypt[7]. Was this one of those copper mines?

Skipper Copper Mine

5.   THE ELDORADO MINE - SINOIA

[7] Now the list of the presents which the Chiefs of Punt brought consisted above all of gold, ivory and frank incense. Copper also is mentioned among the ills..

Evidence came to hand in some detail when this mine was found. Arthur Eyre and early pioneer was tracking a wounded antelope when he came across ancient mine workings near Chinhoyi (Sinoia). The workings were 850 feet long, and varied in width from 10 to 30 feet. and went down some 25 feet. The discovery led to the development of the Eldorado Mine. The finds in the workings were extensive with wooden buckets, iron hoes being amongst the finds. A rough calculation gave a tonnage of at least 20,000 tons of gold ore being mined by the ancient miners.

Locals also verbally noted that their parents and grandparents had been forced to work the mine for the Portuguese. The original owners sank a number of prospecting shafts but were disappointed at the results. The mine eventually was worked on a commercial basis going down some 580 feet but its closeness to the Manyame (Hunyani) river meant that water was a constant threat and had been the cause of the ancient miners not progressing deeper.

The ore is a conglomerate and yielded some rich values at 277dwt per ton but on average was around 65 dwt. Given that the ancient miners had probably worked the richest ore first and that epithermal type impregnation deposits have values that decrease with depth, the ancients would have gained some rich pickings of 65,000[8] troy ounces of gold. So if indeed the Portuguese were the "owners" they certainly had a good investment.

The mine is located on the outskirts of Chinoyi.

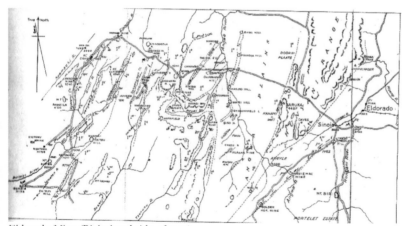

Eldorado Mine (Right hand side of map)

6.   EGGNOG AND EMBIZEMI MINES

---

[8] 20,000 tons of ore multiplied by 65dwt divided by 20 dwt to a troy ounce.

Located in close proximity to Nalatale ruins (No 44) in "The Ancient Ruins of Monomatapa"[9]. The mines were of minor importance if compared to some of the larger mines, but are important in as much as they are close to the Nalatale Ruins. Both mines were started on ancient early surface workings.

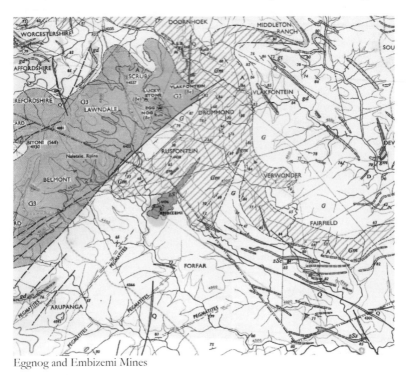

Eggnog and Embizemi Mines

7.   BROKEN LUCK MINE

The mine was located on ancient mine workings three of which were 160, 300 and 190 feet in length. Depth of the ancient working was 20 feet on a quartz reef. Where very high returns were reported. The mine operated from 1901 to 1902 under the Forbes Rhodesia syndicate. Unfortunately the high returns were not disclosed. The total output to 1936 was 7021 ounces of gold from 22,600 tons of ore processed or about 3 ounces per ton.

Loc: 19.03.11 E and 29.52.33 S.

---

[9] The Ancient Ruins of Monomatapa written by the author.

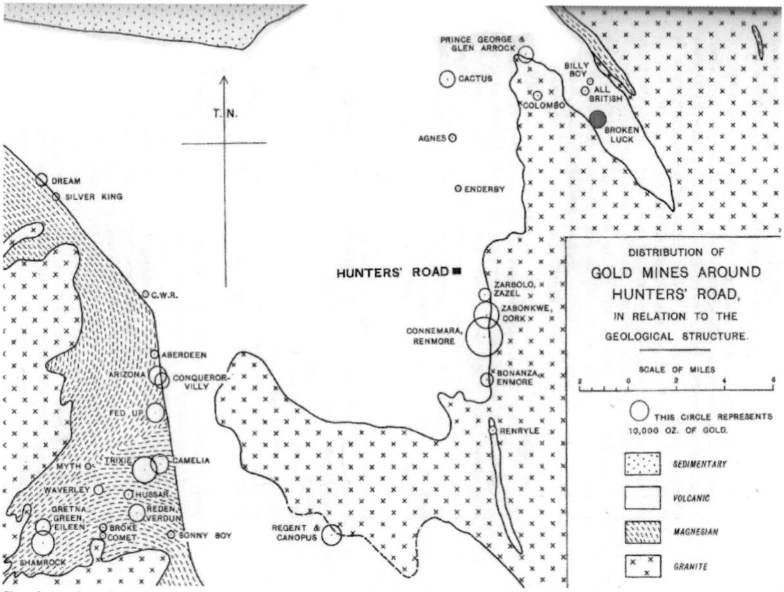
PRINCE GEORGE & GLEN ARROCK
CACTUS
BILLY BOY
ALL BRITISH
COLOMBO
BROKEN LUCK
AGNES
ENDERBY
T.N.
DREAM
SILVER KING
HUNTERS' ROAD
DISTRIBUTION OF
GOLD MINES AROUND
HUNTERS' ROAD,
IN RELATION TO THE
GEOLOGICAL STRUCTURE.
SCALE OF MILES
2 0 2 4 6
THIS CIRCLE REPRESENTS
10,000 OZ. OF GOLD.
SEDIMENTARY
VOLCANIC
MAGNESIAN
GRANITE
ZARBOLO, ZAZEL
ZABONKWE, CORK
CONNEMARA, RENMORE
C.W.R.
ABERDEEN
ARIZONA
CONQUEROR-VILLY
FED UP
BONANZA, ENMORE
RENRYLE
MYTH
TRIXIE
CAMELIA
WAVERLEY
HUSSAR
GRETNA, GREEN, EILEEN
REDEN, VERDUN
BROKE COMET
SONNY BOY
REGENT & CANOPUS
SHAMROCK
Broken Luck mine.

8. CWR MINE

The mine is one mile north of Fort Ingwenya which was built to defend the area in the 1896 rebellion. The mine was located on three lines of ancient workings about 50 yards apart. There are visible on the east side of the mine in the picture below but have subsequently been re-worked which has obliterated any evidence. The fort is below the slight curve in the road amongst a group of trees. The old hunters road ran along the base of the fort which came from Thaba Ziki Mambo, then from Fort Ingwenya went north to Hunter's Road railway siding then over the Kwe Kwe river up to Gatooma. There are still remains of the old road to be seen, namely Hunter's Road siding, Inyathi Mission and through the Matopos.

Loc: 19.10.11 E and 29.35.61 S.

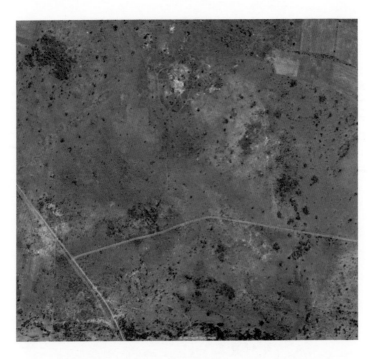

The picture below shows how the ancient line workings have been re-worked.

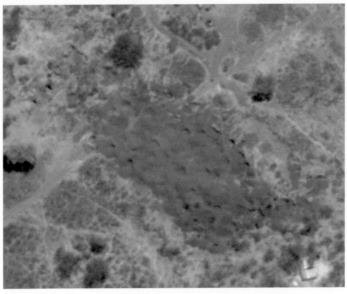

CWR Mine

9.   PETROL AND GOOD SHEPARD MINES

These mines lie in the Gatooma area (Now Kadoma) four main fissures produced 20,000 tons of gold, all were mined under different names but used ancient workings to indicate ore shoots. The mines are in close proximity to the Cam and Motor Mine.

The Cam and Motor Mine is situated 130 km south west of Harare, 10 km to the east of Kadoma, at Eiffel Flats on the site of the former Cam and Motor Mine. The mine was once the largest producer of gold in Zimbabwe and produced in excess of 150 tonnes of gold in its entire life. Three main ore bodies were mined by the Cam and Motor Gold Mining Company, the previous owners of the mine. These were the Motor Lode, Cam Lode and Petrol Lode. In 1968, the mine was closed with the gold price at US$35 per ounce and the mine operating at depths of 1,800 metres when operations were no longer viable. At that stage, the mine cut-off grade was 8 grams per ton and so it was considered likely that there could be significant resources adjacent to the old workings that would now be economic to mine. Rio Zim commissioned an exploration program to search for the expected lower grade zones surrounding the mined ore bodies.

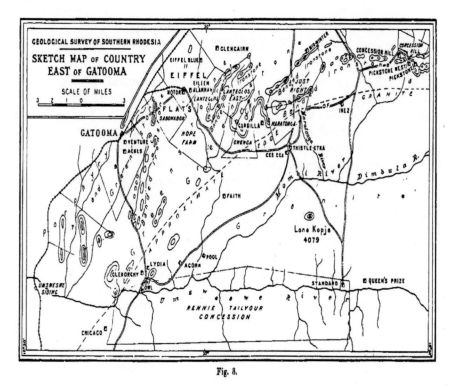

Fig. 3.

10. GRETNA GREEN

The ancients worked a quartz reef lying on the south east side of a bed of banded iron stone. The ancients worked a rich ore shoot sunk on a cross cut to the reef. While the ancients worked the surface further mining in 1917 found over 300 ounces from 173 tons of ore. What occurred on the surface must have been extremely rich in visible gold.

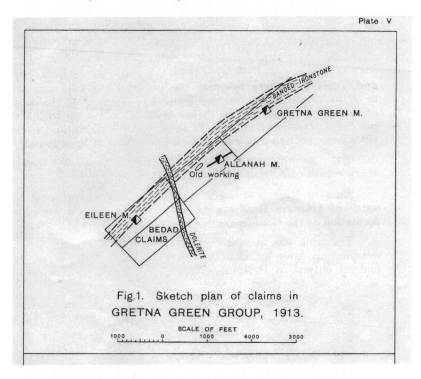

Plate V

Fig.1. Sketch plan of claims in
GRETNA GREEN GROUP, 1913.

SCALE OF FEET

11. EILEEN, ALLANHA AND BEDAD MINES

These mines are grouped together as they occur close to each other. The Bedad claims was worked on rubble, this may have come from the Eileen mine reef which had decomposed and moved over the millennia or from the activities of the ancients who worked the Eileen mine and the Allanha mines. The reef in the location is a quartz buck reef with the gold appearing in offshoots from the buck reef. The ancients mined over 100 feet and this is shown in the map above as "old workings".

12. ZAZEL MINE

The Zazel claims were worked between 1906 and 1909 and had a small output from reef in 1933 included in the returns from the Zarbolo, and some later outputs from cyanidation of tailings. The total output is 325 oz gold from 695 tons of ore, equal to 9.35 dwt per ton. The earlier period the workings on the Zarbolo bocks were at the northern end, where there was an open stope about 80 feet long. The main shaft ,was situated just north of the claim boundary on the Zazel claims, and an air shaft was sunk at the southern end of the working. The body of quartz reef was stated to be about 26 feet wide. Parts of the quartz near the surface were said to be extremely rich , but the values dropped to traces at water level. It appears that the shoot worked was about 100 feet long. The shaft is said to have re-entered ore at the bottom, but the two pumps used by the tributer were unable to cope with the large body of water which came into the shaft.

On the Zazel claims work has been done on two small quartz reefs discovered at the bottom of ancient workings. On one of them a rich shoot about 50 feet long was worked down to water-level where values dropped, but were said to appear to improve a little deeper. This reef dipped at about 45 degrees. In 1933 a small reef striking east and west across the formation and consisting of small overlapping lenticles of quartz was being worked. Recent work is confined to impregnations in banded iron- stone of which there are two bodies, one striking through the Zarbolo and Zazel bocks, and the other through the Cork Mine and the parallel claims to the east of the first line.

13. DICKENS MINE

The Dickens mine holds the title of being the first gold mine to be pegged in the area on the 25th October 1891.
The mine lies 12 miles south west from Masvingo (Fort Victoria) and was pegged on ancient workings. These may not have only been gold workings but also iron from the banded iron stone.
The geologist, Amm who later inspected the mine went on to say that phenomenal values could be obtained from the surface as these were the caps of visible gold that the ancient miners worked. He also confirmed that most gold mines in Zimbabwe had originated from ancient workings.

There are a few mines that were worked to the south east that could have supplied Great Zimbabwe, however as noted in the book " The Ancient Ruins if Monomatapa" mining and stone castle building were not apparently linked as in the richest and biggest ancient mine workings at Kwe Kwe there are only a few small Zimbabwe style ruins. These were certainly not the size one would expect if the gold mining supported the ruins ancient occupants. Then there are some verbal and written examples where the ancient miners were associated with the descendants of today's Shona tribes. Where as the Zimbabwe stone builders appear to be a separate culture.

The art of smelting ore and making iron and gold articles seems to have been appreciated and held in high esteem by the ancient stone builders, rather than be part and parcel of their culture as there are places where kilns are found but no Zimbabwe style ruins and ruins where no gold smelting occurred.

14. THE ABOYNE MINE

The mine is situated on the old Mount Royal Farm . The claim was originally pegged by A. Adams, and later became the possession of the Sable Mining Company. There was considerable evidence of ancient mining by ancients who had mined there. On the western end of the strike, where four skeletons were found withs tone implements. Radio carbon dating showed these to be about 1400 years old. (600 AD).

The mine is in fine basaltic greenstone. The stone hammers found next to the skeletons were made of this rock. The gold was found in blue black quartz in lenticular veins. The reef quartz is glassy in nature with a milky white appearance, with the gold found in association with galena within patches of the quartz.

We are lucky to have a mine engineer record the finds at this mine location, as most mine reports did not note ancient activities.

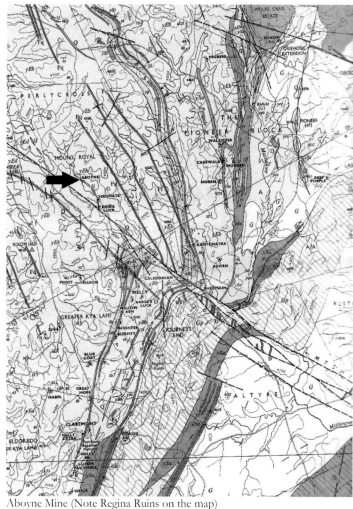

Aboyne Mine (Note Regina Ruins on the map)

15. DHLO DHLO TIN

What is little known is that Dhlo Dhlo ruins were also a center for tin smelting, thought to have been mined on the upper reaches of the Shangani River. A claim was pegged for tin in 1917 but there is no further record of it.

16. MASON MINE

The mine is located on Kya Lami Farm and the reef consisted of three black quartz reefs, the ancients had mined these to a depth of thirty feet. The mine opened up on these workings was not found profitable and after reaching some 125 feet deep the mine closed in 1940.

17. MORSEL MINE

The mine is located on The Pioneer Block on the east bank of the Pangale River. The ancient workings were opened up in 1911 with an inclined shaft that reached 120 feet where the reef split into unpayable stringers. The mine reported outputs in in 1914 averaging 6.3 dwt per ton.

18. PEGGY MINE

Also located on the on Kya Lami Farm the Peggy Mine was first pegged in 1908. The ancient workings consisted of surface diggings. However several shafts were sunk across these ancient workings, chasing quartz reefs 12 to 18 inches wide. The eastern inclined shafts were also sunk on these ancient workings reaching some 400 feet long. 761 ounces of gold were extracted from 2,017 tons mined.

19. THE COPPER DUKE

Copper was mined at the Copper Duke mine by ancients, in a trench some 100 feet long and 38 feet deep. The location is over 14 miles west, south west of Gatooma in a deposit that was very rich in copper. The current mine was sunk over the top of the ancient workings. (See other map – Owl mine)

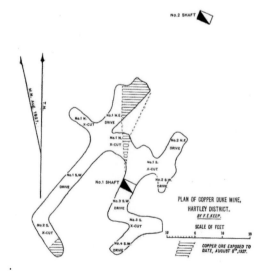

20. THE MAUD MINE

The mine was located on ancient workings, some 2195 tons of ore were taken out yielding 585 ounces of gold. The reef was striking south by east at an angle of 30 degrees for 60 feet. The gold was coarse grained and associated with galena.

21. THE NEW TOPAZ MINE

The mine is located about 7 miles west north west of Battlefields on ground mined by ancients who had opened up the reef for about 200 feet. The gold was found in quartz reefs, with some 45,872 tons of ore being mined which yielded 18,430 ounces of gold. This was just under two and a half ounces of gold per ton of ore.

22. THE SOUTH TAPPERT CLAIMS

Located on the north bank of the Umsweswe River about 7 miles due south of Gatooma, The ancients had "scratched" the surface. The reef of quartz lies on the edge of blue lava. The proximity close to the river meant that water was soon encountered and made the claims unpayable.

23. THE ESPERANZA MINE

A very rich reef was mined by the ancients which led to the establishment of the mine in 1907. A total of 2,037 ounces of gold was produced from 3,850 tons of ore milled. The mine is located 4 miles south west of Umsweswe rail siding.

24. THE DON JUAN MINE

Located on the left bank of the Sesombi river, the mine is surrounded by ancient workings, The reef varied from a few inches to three feet and in places showed visible massive gold. With depth the gold becomes more associated with pyrite and other sulphide minerals. The area today (2020) has been extensively potholed by small miners.

25. THE INVINCIBLE MINE

The mine was first pegged in June 1893, before the downfall of King Lobengula. The reef had been worked to a depth of 50 feet by ancients, when water was struck, this prevented the ancients from digging deeper. Early yield from 1905 to 1911 gave 79,234 ounces of gold from an ore tonnage of 115,578 tons. This was by today's standards exceptionally rich.

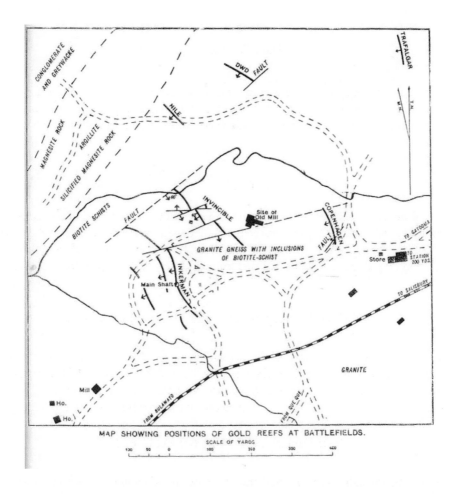

MAP SHOWING POSITIONS OF GOLD REEFS AT BATTLEFIELDS.

SCALE OF YARDS

26. THE HERO MINE

The mine was located on rubble mined by the ancients, which came from several small reefs. The quartz was associated with sulphides and contained some visible gold.

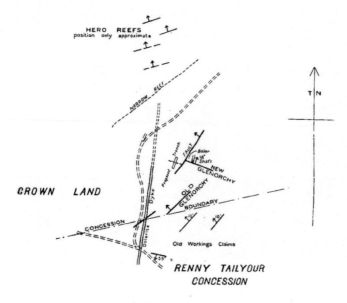

HERO REEFS
position only approximate

CROWN LAND

NARROW REEF

NEW GLENORCHY

OLD GLENORCHY BOUNDARY

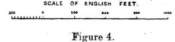

CONCESSION

Old Workings Claims

RENNY TAILYOUR
CONCESSION

Plan of the Glenorchy and neighbouring reefs.

SCALE OF ENGLISH FEET.

Figure 4.

27. THE HOPE MINE

The ancients mined gold here on a reef for some 1000 feet which ran in a north east direction. Little more is known about the mine, which apparently only crushed the rubble from the ancient workings.

28. THE GLADSTONE REEF

A. R. Sawyer noted there were several mines on this reef, however what is interesting about the ancient mine here was that timber supports were used, with standing timber being found 50 feet below the surface. The ancients again came down to the water table and could go no deeper.

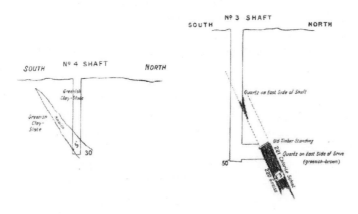

SECTIONS THROUGH GLADSTONE REEF.

by A. R. Sawyer. F.G.S etc.

SCALE: 1 INCH = 20 FEET.

29. THE OLD WORKINGS REEF.

The mine of the same name was found in the Salisbury Gold Field, near the Salisbury Reef, was worked o extensive old workings by the ancients and carried some very rich gold. Not much more information has been found on the reef and mine.

30. THE ANTELOPE MINE REEFS.

The claims were first pegged in 1894 on a long line of ancient workings, the reef consisting of high pyritic quartz and banded iron stone. There was evidence that they had to hurriedly build fortifications along the ridge top to defend their claims. The workings roughly run along the hill ridge and is marked by the red line between the crosses. Claim numbers 4268, 2471, 2447 and 2708 being the most important and were opened up on the ancient workings. Some free gold was visible.

The mine on the old excavations went down some 80 feet. Finds on the 80 foot level included bones of oxen and antelope. Large stone hammers were found and included large granite blocks that would have had to have been carried some distance. These blocks were also found on the surface and could have been used to crush the ore on.

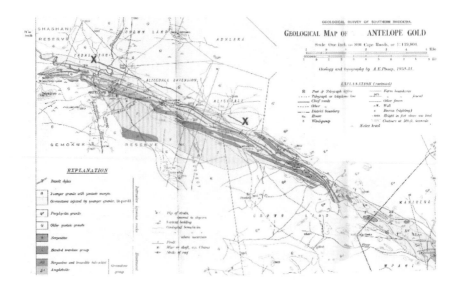

31. THE SIREN MINE.

The mine is located about 500 yards on the left bank of the Gwelo river and was first pegged by Rhodesian Gold Trust Company in 1900 as the Irene Mine. The ancients had worked a line some 2000 feet long , with varying depths. The reef was thin and consisted of a very well developed quartz fissure in granite. Payable values of gold were found to exist down to 400 feet below the ancient workings. The area today is marked by the Leopard mine and other mines close by.

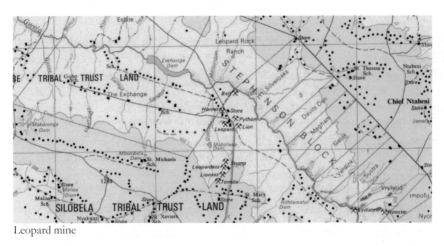

Leopard mine

32. THE CRESCENT MINE

The ancients mined the reef in the shape of a crescent hence the name. The gold was worked in a copper and gold associated gossan, which included some malachite. Pyrite was also found in the material. The Crescent Mine is marked by a red C in the sketch map below. No returns of gold were noted but over 400 tons of copper was later mined by modern equipment (1934).

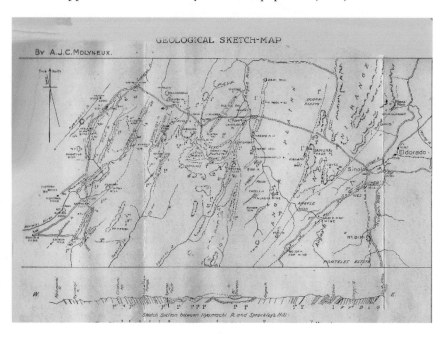

33. GONDIA MINE

The Gondia Mine lies on the southernmost edge of the Piriwiri Mineral Belt. The nearby Biriwiri river and Mount Zumbo providing a refuge and water for the ancients operations. The mine was essentially a copper mine with some gold. The gold ran at 8 dwt per ton which was quite good for those days. The workings ran just below the crest of the hill, with the summit formed by dense quartz. Chalybite, Chalcopyrite and bornite was found in this quartz. (Gondia mine can be located bottom left hand corner of the above sketch plan.)

Siderite or Chalybite

34. ANZAC MINE

The mine is located a few miles north east of the Gondia mine, the ancients mining a quartz reef stained with yellow. The reef is also mixed with hematite. Some copper was also suspected to have been mined by the ancients. The original workings were some 25 feet deep.

35. COMYN RANCH CLUSTER (LOWER GWELO ROAD).

If one looks at the area around Silobela particularly where the bridge crosses the Gwelo river there were a large unprecedented number of ancient workings. The New Stranger mine being one of the mines, Montague mine, Birthday Gift, The Lydiate, The Fed Up mine, The Foundling Mine, The Rooster Mine, Do Me Good and Gothic. All these were located on ancient workings. The Do Me good mine was located on 900 feet of ancient workings, the reef being a narrow lenticular reef vein containing galena, stibnite, and pyrite. The Fondling Mine was opened up on 500 feet of ancient workings,

36. LEOPARD MINE GROUP

Close to the Comyn cluster lies a group of ancient working centered around the Leopard Mine. The Leopardess, Belt, Python, Lion, Stump and Termite Mines form up the group. The Leopard Mine was sunk on ancient working some 1000 feet long, the ancients washing the crushed quartz in the Gwelo river. The mine was started in 1898 and values ran at about 8dwt per ton of gold ore. An early cross section of the mine shows the extent of the ancient workings, which reached some 50 feet below ground level. See below.

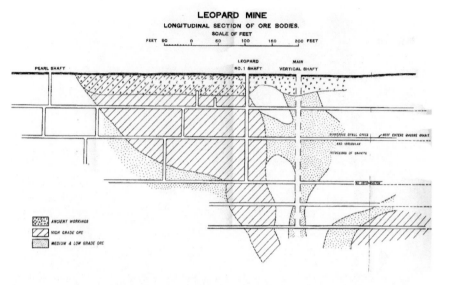

37. GOTHIC, PAGAMESA AND DO ME GOOD MINES.

The ancients mined three reefs in this area close to the west bank of the Gwelo/Gweru river.

Each mine was located on a separate reef of quartz but all in close proximity to each other. Apart from gold later mining was for antimony. A total of 34,715 ounces of gold was mined in the three reefs, which were largely worked out by 1934.

38. THE GELDENHUYS DEEP

The ancients worked rubble from a quartz reef with little depth. The rubble was said have a high value of gold which was treated with modern technology to yield some 14,068 ounces of gold. The claim is located just east of the Gothic mine complex, but on the east bank of the Gweru river.

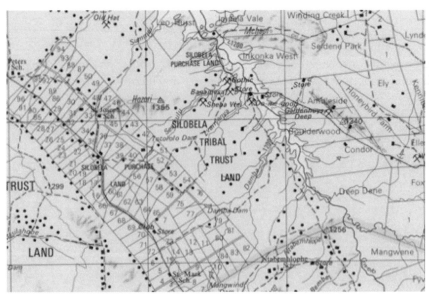

Geldenhys Deep Mine

39. THE GOLD ENOUGH MINE (ESQUIRE MINE)

Located between the Gothic cluster of mines and the Geldenhuys Deep, , the mine was located on ancient workings running some 1300 feet. Some 870 ounces of gold was worked until the mine was closed down.
It lies on the norther boundary of the Condor farm (see map above).

40. THE ODD FELLOW MINE

Also located on the Condor farm lies the Odd Fellow mine, which was located on 120 feet of ancient workings. The gold averaged about 3dwt per ton of ore mined.

41. BLUE JACKET MINE - TATI

Mary Lippert wrote that she visited the mine in the 1890 and noted that it was started on a line of ancient workings in the Tati Gold Belt. The mine can be seen today and has been extensively mined.
The mine lies west of the old township of Tati and within the Tati gold belt. The mine was named after Blue Jacket Anderson an early miner who had prospected in Australia, who wore an old blue denim jacket. The main street in Francistown is name after him.

According to records, Mzilikazi, the Matabele king, did not agree to sell the land to the Europeans prospectors, but rather preferred to give them permission to extract gold and other minerals.

With permission to prospect and mine granted, Old Tati was transformed into the site for the first gold rush in Southern Africa and the mineral boom led to the growth of the town or commercial center between 1868 and 1870.

Blue Jacket Mine

42. THE NOURSE MINE

Located in the old Victoria Native Reserve (now open titled land) and near the Munongo School, the mine was worked on ancient surface workings. Little else was reported other than 1957 grades were 7.7 dwt to the ton.

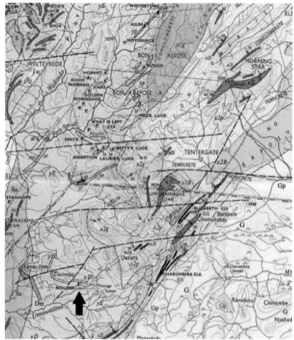
Nourse Mine

43. SUMMERTON MINE

This gold mine is better known for a massive area of dolly holes on a small granite outcrop where extensive gold quartz crushing occurred. The gold is thought to have come from the area now known as the Summerton Mine. The grade was 8.3 dwt per ton when the mine was working.

Dolly holes

44. THE FORTUNATE MINE

The mine is situated close to the old Nooitgedacht farmhouse. The gold was found in solid grey quartz formed against a body of pinkish quart which contained visible gold. The ancients had spread rubble over 4 acres, which was later exploited by trenching, Three shafts were later dug which ran along ancient workings which went down a few feet taking advantage of rich ore. The total output in 1933 on the old workings was 973 tons of ore which yielded 97 ounces of gold.

Gold in pink quartz

Fortunate and Summerton Mine locations

45. THE SUFFOLK MINE

About a 1000 meters from the Ngezi River the Suffolk mine was founded on seven trenches of ancient working over a length of 1000 feet.. Shallow shafts or deep trenches were sunk on these ancient workings to a depth of 22 feet. The gold bearing rock is blue quartz which had values of 65 dwt per ton over 5 inches. The mine produced 2464 tons of ore from crushing which yielded 545 ounces of gold (1912 to1913).

46. THE CORNWALLIS MINE

The mine is situated 1¼ miles south-west of the Dopie mine on the old Kromdraai farm.

The mine was owned by E. Frankis, who produced during 1917 and 1918. The ground was re-pegged in 1935 by A. R. Ready and tributed to J. C. Trounce in 1937. Gold was produced during 1936. R. A. Duthie re-pegged the ground in 1940 and produced gold during 1941. J. C. Cameron stated in 1917 that the reef was faulted in No. 1 shaft, 45 feet deep, while in No. 2 shaft, at the same depth, the reef had an average width of 30 inches. Although good results were found in the pan, long pieces of copper pyrites and galena were also present. The ancients worked the reef to a depth of 35 feet over a strike of 160 feet. The two shafts are 110 feet apart.

The reef was 35 inches wide with visible gold found along the footwall. The gold averaged 3 dwt per ton.

47. THE COLD PUNCH MINE

Located 5 miles south east of Belingwe, the mine was first pegged in 1933 by J.M. Harris. The ancients had worked a reef for some 300 feet and to depth of 109 feet. Values for thew mine ran between 15 to 40 dwt per ton. Little else is given about the mine but it is worth mentioning that given the proximity to asbestos fiber that the ancients used fiber in their pottery to increase its heat retention capability. So in the Belingwe area the ancients had access to gold, iron ore and asbestos fiber, all used in manufacturing basic wares and ornaments.

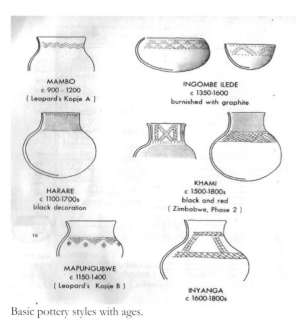

Basic pottery styles with ages.

48. B AND B MINE

Located 7 miles south west of Belingwe, the mine was first pegged in 1907, on a reef worked by ancients. Evidently the mine was only worked in 1907 and 1908. The reef proved to be poor at any depth and little else is noted.

The Belingwe area where gold is found consists of two types of rock, gold associated with banded iron stone and gold associated with greenstone. The banded iron stone gold seems to have been more utilized and identified for mining than the greenstone by ancients.

49. C MINE

The mine was first pegged by Europeans in 1907, along ancient workings on a 3000 foot long formation of quartz. Some rich sections were found that contained much visible gold. Reports noted that 600 dwt over 6 inches were found and in many cases over 300 dwt were found on the reef. A dolerite shelf or sill seems to have forced the precipitation of gold from solution into the quartz.

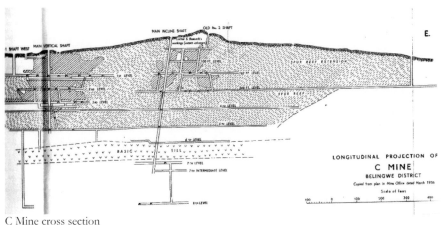

C Mine cross section

The total production as at 1912 was 28,937 ounces of gold from 220,749 tons milled.

50. THE BLUE BELL MINE

The reef had become exposed on the surface as a large blow and was some 12 feet wide. The ancients had worked the foot wall side of the reef taking out reef

12 to 18 inches wide, but had failed to descend or expose any further payable reef. One wonders at this as would hardly seem viable to even undertake that little work, so there may have been ground rubble taken instead for crushing.

51. THE BUNYIP CLAIMS

These claims cover the mines called the Southern Cross, Robin Hood, Simbi and Franklin mines.

They are in flat country in which the Nuanetsi River has cut a narrow valley, A. E. Phaup reported on the mine in 1951 as follows: "The earliest work on the group was done on the Robin Hood which is about 200 yards from the Wanezi drift. The claims were acquired by Rhodesia Ltd. in 1913 and tributed to Granger Bros., who milled ore from 1914 to 1916. The sands were cyanided in 1926-7.

The claims were taken over by the London & Rhodesian Mining and Land Co. Ltd., in 1922 and were subsequently allowed to go to forfeiture.

There are two or more lines of ancient workings about 20 to 30 feet deep, on narrow white veins of quartz which dip almost vertically in schist. The quartz is almost free from sulphides and unlike the other reefs, is said to be free milling. The Grangers worked a series of short shoots of ore to a depth of about 220 feet, but do not seem to have explored all the ancient workings on the parallel reefs.

A little later E. Bosch worked the Franklin mine, which is about a quarter of a mile NE. of the Bunyip reef and about 75 yards north of the old coach road. The area is covered with rubble of white and grey quartz which is said to carry about 1 dwt. gold per ton, and through the rubble an east-west 'buck' reef outcrops. On the south side of the buck reef is a line of ancient workings over 50 yards long which dips at about 60 degrees south. Under them a quartz vein up to 30 inches wide has been exposed with a granite or felsitic schist hanging-wall and a buck reef footwall. It is said to carry patchy values and to pan up to 5 dwt. per ton. It is thought that the gold shoot pitches to the west. There are .several shallow shafts on or near the ancient workings but no serious mining has been done.

The Bunyip claims were pegged by R. R. White and transferred to Mrs. F. M. Kennedy in 1933. The Kennedys and their partners Bunyip Mines Ltd., worked on no less than nine blocks of claims during the period 1933 to 1943.

The following are further extracts from Phaup's report:-"It is said that from 1933 to 1935 the outputs came mostly from rubble and after that from various reefs and rubble".

The Southern Cross reef, according to Phaup, is about a quarter of a mile north-east of the Bunyip reef and is said to have first been opened up by the Granger Bros. The Kennedys and their partners worked the reef between 1939 and 1942. The workings are now inaccessible. The reef was a fairly narrow quartz vein with gneissic granite on the hanging-wall and a light greenstone schist on the foot-wall. It contained some very rich patches in the oxidized zone and was refractory in the sulphides zone, where it contained much pyrites and pyrrhotite and some chalcopyrite. The average gold content was not high and is said to have been poor in the bottom of the mine. The reef had a strike of about 100 feet and dipped at 45 degrees northwest. The ore shoot seems to have had a gentle pitch to the south-west and was stoped completely to the bottom of the vertical shaft which was 120 feet deep. In recent years J. Masefield explored the ancient working over 100 feet long when goes down at 45 degrees south-west to about 100 feet. The ancient working is 5 feet wide on the surface but soon narrows to about 18 inches and is filled with surface wash. The reef is 3 to 18 inches wide and is a vein of white quartz stained with ochre and dips 45 degrees south-west between the hanging-wall of granite and a foot-wall of folded light green schist. For about 10 feet near the beginning of the 90 foot (vertical) level the hanging-wall is " buck" reef and at the face there are barren quartz stringers in the granite lying parallel to the quartz reef which is said to pay 10 dwt. over 6 inches.

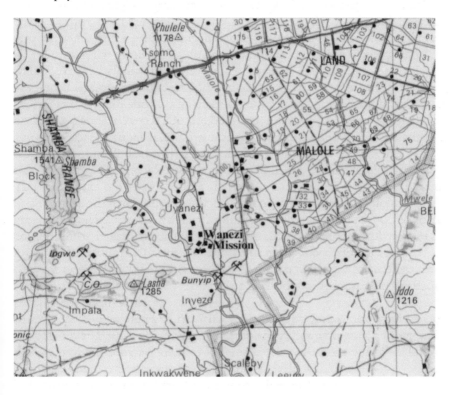

52. THE ROSINA CLAIMS

The Rosina claims are situated about 500 yards west of the Hope mine on Impala farm. They were worked by A. H. Bell and Normand during 1912 and 1913. The reef is from 15 to 20 inches wide. The formation is schist which is considerably disturbed. An adit was sunk at an angle of 5 to 10 degrees, the incline has been driven for some 300 feet on the small reef. A small shoot of values was found at the adit entrance and a limited amount of underhand stoping was done for about 60 feet. A sample collected in the face assayed 2.2 dwt. over 36 inches. There was also a line of old workings across the claims, and panning's show values of 8 to 10 dwt.

53. THE SIRUS MINE

The Sirius Mine is situated on New Eldorado Farm, about one and a half miles south of the Claremont Mine, and on the same strike. Here a line of ancient stopes went down to 50 feet.

The mine first recorded an output in 1922. In 1931, it was reopened by four shafts. Values were reported as being lower than the first output, and the mine was worked intermittently until 1938. After the war the main inclined shaft was sunk to 210 feet and the Lenticular nature of the reef seemed to be changing to one of a more consolidated character. The lenses were three to four feet in length, with values from one to 10 ounces per ton, but the average over the drive width was only 3 dwt. per ton.

In 1946, a new ore body was located on one of the adjacent blocks. This led to the prospecting of 500 feet of the strike, but only 75 per cent. of this length was payable. An old inclined shaft ,vas deepened from 53 to 65 feet, but, apart from ancient fillings down to 20 feet, which panned up to 7 dwt. per ton, little of value was found.

An ore body was found on Sirius 5 Block and prospected for 300 feet. It was found to be an over pegging of a block held by the owners of the Nelly 404 and 405 blocks, and work had to cease.

The mine was closed as being uneconomic in 1947. Interest has still been maintained in the property, and the farm and owner has from time to time explored the workings, but with little success.

The reef consists of small quartz lenses striking north east and dipping at about 65 degrees west. The reef is conformed to the cleavage of the country rock, which is a carbonated chlorite schist, often mineralized with pyrite.

54. THE NEW ECLIPSE MINE

The mine was first pegged on ancient workings. There is no further mention of the ancient workings however the mining report goes on to note:
The New Eclipse Mine is situated on Battle Farm, about one mile north west of Shangani. It was the deepest mine in the area and reputed to be, when it was working, the deepest small worker's mine in the whole of Southern Africa. It was 2,000 feet deep and worked on 17 levels. The claims first belonged to the Bembesi District Gold Claims Ltd., which did a considerable amount of shaft-sinking before 1908. The claims were repegged by J. R. Stewart. Production commenced in 1908 and continued without a break until 1926. After this period sands and slimes only were treated up to 1939. In 1936, a company, J. R. Stewart and Sons Ltd., was formed and worked the dumps until the mine closed. Small pockets of reef were found in the underground working but they were not payable and the continued re-treatment of the dumps kept the mine working till 1943.
The reef is a persistent vein of white quartz dipping west, striking north and making an angle of 45 degrees with the cleavage of the country rock, which is a chlorite schist. Both the schist and quartz were reputed to carry gold. Reports give the width of the reef to be eight inches, in a three-to 40 foot ore channel. C. R. Stewart, the owner of Battle Farm, who worked in the mine, gives a width of reef much less than this. Though small, it was very rich. The strike developed was over 1,800 feet and contained three pay shoots, a north, a central and a south shoot. The three together had a strike length of 700 feet on the 2nd and 3rd levels. On the 6th level, a strong fault cuts obliquely across the ore channel at 200 feet north of the main shaft, and has a lateral displacement of 25 feet with a pronounced bend in the reef on the northern side. On the 5th level, only a bend in the ore channel is visible. The wall-rocks of the pay shoots are heavily carbonated, but in the barren zone on the 4th level they consist of a younger uncarbonated doleritic greenstone dyke. On the 5th level south the wall rocks were reported to be composed of schistose porphyry. Samples of this sheared porphyry can be found on the dumps. The reef is known to narrow occasionally and become unpayable, but at these points there is a tendency for the fissure to steepen to about 70 degrees. Thus the pay shoots were located in the flatter parts of the shear-zone.
In 1939, dewatering down to the 7th level located pockets of low-grade ore on the 3rd, 4th and 5th levels. These were stoped out but with poor returns, and cyaniding of the dumps continued. There are few reports on the upper levels and there seem to be no reports on the lower levels. Thus there is no information on the character of the reef or values in depth.

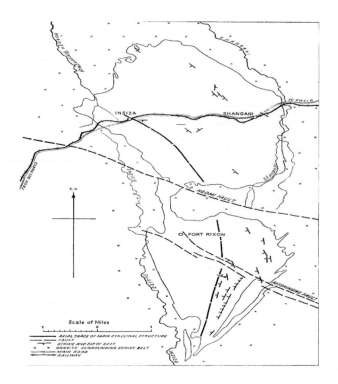

55. ANNIES LUCK MINE

The evidence here of ancient mining was the finding of ancient workings in the mine shafts. The report reads:

There were two distinct reefs, a foot-wall of hard, close-grained quartz and a hanging wall reef of white quartz. They lie in the same zone of mineralization as the Nelly Reef and form an east parallel body. The two reefs lie almost next to each other and strike about N20E. and dip 65 degrees west. The country rock is greenstone schist. The foot-wall reef was wide, but the hanging wall reef was narrow and erratic. In a winze below the 83-foot level the hanging wall leader was lenticular and lay across the fissure.

The mine was opened by two shafts, a vertical in the hanging wall and an incline on the reef down to 83 feet. At this level the two shafts were connected by a drive 65 feet long. In both shafts ancient workings were found down to 30 feet. A winze was sunk for 20 feet in the north end of the drive and the hanging wall reef sampled. Although good in the drive, samples in the winze were poor, only a half dwt. per ton.. The footwall reef also proved disappointing.

The total output, including gold from the treatment of sands and limes, was 407 ounces of gold from 1,674 tons of ore, an average recovery of 4.9 dwt. per ton.

56. THE BLIGHTY MINE

The Blighty Mine was situated on Greater Kya Lami Farm, East South East. of the homestead. A banded ironstone forms a prominent ridge in this section of the farm and, in its footwall, which dips west at angles between35 and 50 degrees, are lenses of blue auriferous quartz. Two gold shoots have been located and have been developed along a strike of 350 feet. The ancients mined the lenses in the banded ironstone.

The mine was opened by a vertical shaft, intersecting the lode at 80 feet, with a drive north-east for 35 feet. This drive was connected by a stope to a surface incline running across the reef to follow the pitch of the ore shoot. The shoot pitches north at 30 degrees but has a strike length of only 20 to 30 feet. On the 80-foot level the quartz stringer is only an inch wide but gradually improves to form six to 12-inch lenses as the pay zone is reached. The mine was very rich down to 40 feet, but below this level payable values were infrequent. No stoping of the sulphide ore was done because of low values, and mining was confined to the oxidized zone. Opencast workings for a further 400 feet along the strike failed to reveal anything more than patchy values.

From 1919to 1923, the grade of the ore was good and 1,068 ounces of gold were extracted from 789 tons of ore, an average recovery of almost one and a half ounces per ton. During this period a further 125 ounces were extracted by treatment of 850 tons of sands. From 1934 to 1944, the mine was worked almost continually, with a break for two years in 1936and 1937. During this period 1,124 ounces of gold were extracted from 9,795 tons of ore, and a further 179 ounces from the retreatment of 5,802 tons of sands and slimes, an average recovery of 2.7 dwt. per ton. The reef worked in the 1920s was the original Blighty reef, but the reef worked in the 1930s was a parallel reef 150 feet to the east.

57. THE CHROMATE MINE

The mine was opened by two inclined shafts, No. 1 lying to the north of No. 2. Ancient workings were found, one lying between the two shafts and one 80 feet south of No. 2 shaft. These ancient workings suggest two ore shoots, one north and one south of No. 2 shaft. In 1936, No. 1 shaft was inaccessible but No. 2 was 100 feet down on the dip of the reef. A level was driven at 80 feet for about 50 feet to the north, to prove the reef, which carried mixed sulphides. Gold values varied, though some rich ore was found. By 1936, most of the oxidized ore had been stoped and very little work in the sulphide zone was attempted. Nevertheless, the mine continued to produce small outputs for a further three years, from 1938 to 1940.

The total output was 370 ounces of gold from 2,178 tons of ore, an average recovery of 3.4 dwt. per ton

58. SHAMROCK AND ROSE OF SHARON MINES

Shamrock and Rose of Sharon Mines, situated about a mile from the Gwelo river on the old Ranche farm, comprise two or three long lines of reef which were marked by ancient workings, and attracted attention in the early days. The reefs were purchased for 200,000 Pounds, mainly in shares, and developed by the Rose of Sharon and Shamrock Gold Mining Company, Limited, between1900 and 1904. Early reports give some useful information about the properties. The reefs strike a little north of east and dip in southerly directions. The claims are cut by a dolerite dyke as shown by the map. East of the dyke the Shamrock reef dips at approximately 71 degrees. The Rose of Sharon reef outcrops 370 feet north of the Shamrock and dips at about 48 degrees in the same direction. If the reefs continue at the same angles they should meet at a point 360 feet south-south-east of the old main shaft at a depth of about 675 feet. The outcrop of the Rose of Sharon reef curves and 400 feet west of the shaft the two reefs are only about 140 feet apart. A length of 600 feet of reef was developed on the Rose of Sharon, and about 750 feet on the Shamrock reef. In the western section only one reef was developed; this has a similar strike to the Shamrock reef, but offset some 200 feet farther north.

59. CAMELIA MINE

The Camelia Mine is situated in the southwestern part of the area partly on Keynshamburg farm and partly on Somerset Estate. The ore body is a quartz reef striking north-east. and south-wrest and dipping veltically or steeply to the northwest.

The mine was located on two ancient workings 90 feet apart, of which the south-western one was about 100 feet long, and the northeastern one 50 feet long.

A mill was in operation on the claims from 1913 to 1916, and in 1917 an unstated quantity of ore ,vas crushed at the Trixie mill with ore from that mine. The Camelia dumps have been retreated subsequently. The recorded tonnage is 22,269 tons crushed yielding 7,823 oz gold, equal to 7.0 dwt per ton.

There is little to be seen besides dumps and an old open stope. The north-western, or hanging wall of this stope is formed of a white sericite schist, but the weathered rock on the dumps is a hard black biotite schist. The mine was reported on several times by the Resident Mining Engineer and his assistants, from whose reports and mine sections the following information is taken. The greater part of the ore milled ,vas taken from the northeast portion of the reef. Reports about the time the mine closed down showed that the reef had been mined on a length of 270 feet to a maximum depth of 220 feet with small stoped portions. The average width was approximately 4 feet. The main incline shaft was sunk to a depth of 400 feet, but the reef pinched out on the foot wall at about 300 feet. At 300 feet a 67 foot cross-cut into the foot wall country showed only stringers of quartz. A little driving was done on one of these, but no values were found. A 33 foot cross cut into the hanging wall at the same depth disclosed no reef.

60. THE SEBAKWE MINE

The Sebakwe Mine was situated on the north bank of the Sebakwe river between the main road and the range of jaspilite hills to the west. The mine was worked in 1911,1924 and1925. Nine hundred and sixty tons of ore were crushed, yielding 614 ounces worth 2,579 Pounds, a return of 12.5 dwt per ton. The ore body is stated to have been a quartz reef upon which there were ancient workings striking north and. south . The reef had a westerly dip of about 80 degrees, and was traced by trenches and old workings for a length of 2,000 feet. The reef is stated in a report to have averaged 36 inches in width and 10dwt in value, but the small tonnage crushed does not bear out this statement.

61. THE KINGS MINE

The King's Mine was previously pegged as the Iona, is situated on Woodlands farm about six miles east northeast of Kwe Kwe. The mine was worked between 1912 and 1914 with a five stamp mill. Three thousand, nine hundred and twenty nine tons were crushed and 5,390 tons cyanided, yielding according to the returns 2,981 ounces of fine gold worth 12,545 Pounds, a return of 15.3dwt per ton.

The mine was pegged on shallow ancient workings in a quartz reef in granite country and about 200 feet long. The strike is east to west, and the dip about 64 degrees. Good values were met from the surface to about 60 feet where the ore became poorer. In a report dated September 1912, it states that on the 100 foot level the reef averaged 4dwt over 31 inches for a distance of 128 feet.

62. THE OWL MINE

The Owl Mine, situated on the north bank of the Umsweswe river, 9 miles south east of Gatooma, was one .of the first mines to be located in the area, being pegged in 1891 before the grant of the Rennie Tailyour Concession, (Umsweswe River block), which now surrounds the claims. The claims were located on two very deep ancient workings .about 50 feet apart. One can deduce here that deep was between 150 and 300 feet, with the ancients hitting the water table effectively stopping their mining.

Some prospecting but no mining appears to have been done on the claims, until Mr. Rolfe, who was then working the Chicago, tributed them and located the reef in 1911. The tribute was .renewed annually until the mine closed down in 1929. On the Owl claims 211,217 tons were crushed, yielding 117,233 oz of gold worth 492,379 Pounds a return of 11.1 dwt per ton with a fineness of .872. On the Owl Extension 4,749 tons yielded 17,765 oz of gold worth 74,61 Pounds, a return of 7.4 dwt. per ton.

The ore body is a quartz reef striking northwest to southeast in gneissic granite with greenstone inclusions, and dipping approximately 33 degrees to the north east. 'The reef occupies a well defined fissure, with a strong slickened sided foot-wall. It varies in thickness from 2 feet upwards to 10 feet. The ore-shoot pitches about due north in plain, or about 40 degrees north of. the direction of dip of the reef.

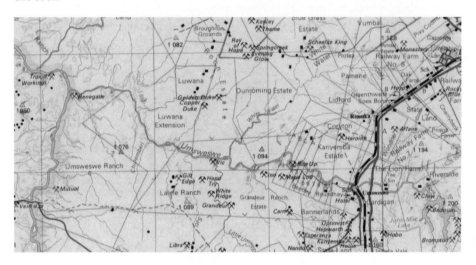

63. THE CUSCO MINE

The Cusco Mine on Ellesmere farm (Main Belt Block) is a little north of the road leading from the homestead on Woodcrest farm to the Veracity Mine. It was worked formerly by the Enterprise Gold Mining and Estates Company Limited in 1908 and 1909. In 1919 and 1920 a small tonnage was milled and the tailings re-treated. The property was again pegged in 1936 and has been producing small outputs since then. The Naomi Mine, about a quarter of a mile to the north, has also been worked with the Cusco.

The ore body of the Cusco Mine lies in the continuation of the Magnesian System. The reef is a quartz vein dipping towards the north-west at a varied angle. It has been opened up by means of two main incline shafts on the reef at 50 feet, 90 feet and 140 feet. Good values were obtained above water level at the 50 foot level over a strike of about 130 feet. On the 90 foot level the best values are confined to a length of strike of about 100 feet. On the 140 foot level the reef is lenticular and narrows in places to a few inches only. The average width of reef matter in the drive is only about half that in the upper levels, but the values appear to be fairly good.

Opposite the pay shoot the wall rocks are composed of massive pale green jointed rock probably greenstone. In the drive west at the intermediate level above the 90 foot level the fissure runs into micaceous schist and the reef pinches to a clay seam and the dip flattens from about 70 degrees to about 50 degrees. The face of the drive looks most promising. The " pinch" pitches towards the north-east at a fairly flat angle. It is possible that the ore shoot also pitches towards the north- east. The values are still good in the east end of the drive at the 140-foot level. This should be continued with a view to establishing the possibility of the shoot pitching north-east. H this is the case larger widths and a longer strike should be obtained at the 140-foot level.

A little prospecting is being done on some ancient workings about 150 yards to the north-east of the Cusco. Operations are considerably impeded by the heavy overburden of soil six to eight feet thick. Several reefs have been exposed, but these are very irregular and appear to be infillings along a series of joint planes. The sulfide minerals, pyrite and galena, are similar to those in the Cusco Mine reef. These claims were formerly worked with the Cusco as the Narran, but no separate output has been declared.

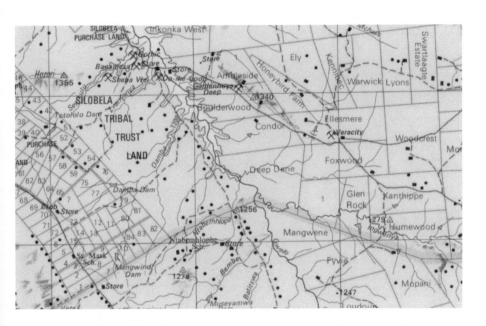

64. THE ELEPHANT MINE

The Elephant Mine is on Stephenson A Block (Gweru river) two miles north-west from the Siren Mine. The claims were originally pegged before 1900 on a very extensive though discontinuous line of ancient workings running east and west in granite.

The strike has since been prospected at intervals for a considerable distance, but insufficient work has been done to establish whether or not the reef is continuous. The greatest depth reached in the workings is about sixty feet. From what can be seen of the reef at present, it appears to be a series of short quartz lenses with general characteristics very similar to those at the Siren Mine.

The mine produced from 1936 to 1937, 1,515 tons of ore being milled for 258 oz. of gold, a return of 3.4 dwt. per ton.

An early gold mine

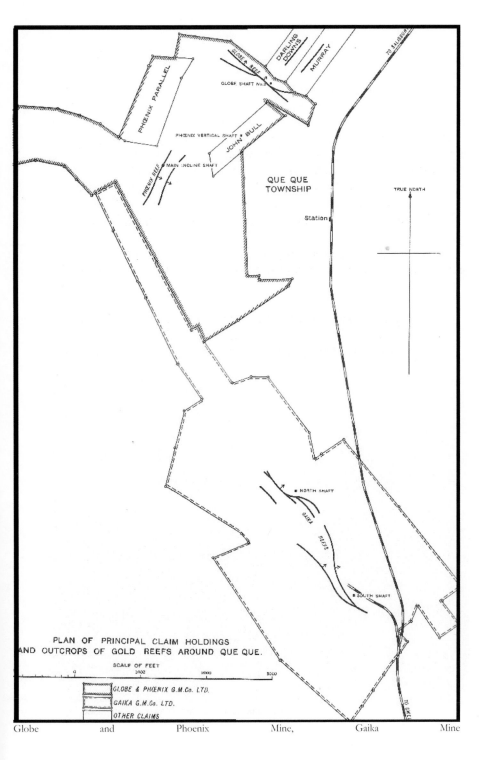

TRUE NORTH

PHOENIX PARALLEL

GLOBE REEF

DARLING DOWNS

MURRAY

TO SALISBUR...

GLOBE SHAFT No.2

PHŒNIX VERTICAL SHAFT

JOHN BULL

PHOENIX REEF ⬛ MAIN INCLINE SHAFT

QUE QUE
TOWNSHIP

Station

⬛ NORTH SHAFT

GAIKA

REEFS

⬛ SOUTH SHAFT

PLAN OF PRINCIPAL CLAIM HOLDINGS
AND OUTCROPS OF GOLD REEFS AROUND QUE QUE.

SCALE OF FEET

0   1000   2000   3000

GLOBE & PHŒNIX G.M.Co. LTD.

GAIKA G.M.Co. LTD.

OTHER CLAIMS

TO GWEL...

Globe   and   Phoenix   Mine,   Gaika   Mine

65. ABOUT THE AUTHOR

Geoffrey Alp is a qualified forensic auditor, governance expert and keen historian. His parents were both keen rock hounds, which is where much of the information used in the book came from Geoffrey also authored the book "The Uncomfortable Truth". An in depth study of the two Rhodesian Viscount tragedies, where he disputed the claims that the Viscounts were shot down with the ground to air Sam 7 missile.
Geoffrey's other book "The Ancient Ruins of Monomatapa" details many of the Zimbabwe style ruins which were constructed between 1100 AD and 1600 AD. This gives an insight into the past of Zimbabwe.

Printed in Great Britain
by Amazon

83043847R00031